The Gun-Runner's Daughter

The Gun-Runner's Daughter

Poems by

Susan Castillo Street

Kelsay Books

© 2018 Susan Castillo Street. All rights reserved. This material may not be reproduced in any form, published, reprinted, recorded, performed, broadcast, rewritten or redistributed without the explicit permission of Susan Castillo Street. All such actions are strictly prohibited by law.

ISBN: 978-1-947465-58-9

Kelsay Books
Aldrich Press
www.kelsaybooks.com

To my brother and sister

    Richard Duncan, 1938-2012
    Sallye Parsons, 1940-2017

May the circle be unbroken.

Acknowledgments

Some of the poems in this volume have appeared in the following reviews and anthologies:

Picaroon: "The Gun-Runner's Daughter," and "Ambrosia"
Prole: "Lines of Desire"
Clear Poetry: "The Alchemist," "Captive," and "Personal"
York Mix: "Closet"
Southern Quarterly: "Rita the Walking Doll"
Poetry Space: "Jesse Garon," "The Peacock's Song," and "Bordello"
Ink Sweat & Tears: "Shelling Peas," "Lucy," and "Under the Volcano"
Poetry Shed: "Hurler," and "What Every Mother Knows"
The Yellow Chair Review: "Animal Magic"
(*Into the Dark* anthology: "Werewolf"
Three Drops in a Cauldron: "Salem"
Chronicles of Eve, Paper Swans Press: "Tightrope Walker"
Ledbury Poetry Festival, *Fantastic Beasts:* "Basilisk," and "Salamander"
The High Window: "Net," and "Permanent Damage"
Noble Dissent anthology: "Harriet Jacobs"
A Face in the Mirror, a Hook on the Door: An Anthology of Urban Legends & Modern Folklore (Three Drops Press): "Revenge"
Ground: "Churchgoer"
Algebra of Owl: "Blue Baby"
The Fat Damsel: "Aftermath"
Atrium: "Cottonmouth," and "A Bibliophile's Vision of Heaven,"
The Lake: "Trove," and "Palimpsest"
Smeuse, "Life Model"
Worcester Remembrance Day Anthology, "Jack Kipling's Medals Speak"
The Writers' Café, "Petticoats"

Contents

I.

Net	17
Aftermath	18
Blue Baby	19
The Alchemist	20
Cottonmouth	21
Permanent Damage	23
Closet	24
Heaven	25
Trove	27
No Wonder I Hate Films	28
Rita the Walking Doll	29
Petticoats	30
Jesse Garon	31
Ambrosia	32
Shelling Peas	33
Err with Verve	34
Hurler	35
Bomb Threats	36
Flight Map	37
Etymology	38
Taxi	39
Tightrope Walker	40
What Every Mother Knows	41
I Won't	42

II.

Salem	45
Werewolf	48
Basilisk	49

Salamander	50
Lucy	51
Jack Kipling's Medals Speak	52
Harriet Jacobs	53
Make America Great Again	54
Revenge	55

III

Lines of Desire	59
Animal Magic	60
A Bibliophile's Vision of Heaven	61
Fundamental	62
Don'ts	63
Bordello	64
Kouros	65
Greensleeves	66
The Peacock's Song	67
Heart: An Assay	68
Under the Volcano	69
Palimpsest	70
Regrets	71
Mixed Border	72
Knowing	73
Way Out	74
Churchgoer	75

About the Author

The Gun-Runner's Daughter

It was a strange old year.
We moved to Oklahoma one day
without warning, and I started a new school.

The teacher taught me to do sums,
I'll give her that. Still, she rabbitted on and on
about my lack of tidiness

until one morning I arrived
and every object in my desk
was strewn across the floor.

"It's to teach you a lesson," she said,
"Nice girls should be tidy!"
I picked it all up, lips pressed tight.

I hope she found my silence scary.
Shortly thereafter, we left town when Dad made headlines:
LOCAL MAN RUNS GUNS TO CUBAN REBELS.

Perhaps I taught my teacher
sometimes it's a waste of effort
to try to place things in neat boxes.

I.

Net

I am three years old.
Outside the house, the old magnolia tree
stretches high into the sky.
Foot on branch,
hand over hand
I climb up toward the clouds,
believe that I can fly,
breathe in the thick perfume
of floating waxy blooms.
From the second-floor window
my father looks out,
sees my reckless grin,
blanches, races downstairs,
stands there tall between the roots
I know he'll always catch me
if I fall.

Aftermath

After the hurricane, things were different.
Grandmother's frame outbuildings had collapsed.
The lights were off, so we burned candles.

When the roads opened, we went for a drive
to Cameron, down on the coast. It used to be a town.
A tidal wave slammed in, dragged houses out into the Gulf,

left rotting bodies dotted through the swamps.
Not many people left. Mosquitoes, though, were rife.
I put an arm outside and suddenly

it pulsed black with teeming insect life. The snakes
came out as well. I had to watch out
where I walked. But I was nine years old and loved the candlelight,

the dark, the fright, the flickering parlour, full of mud and silt.
I drew stick figures with grinning faces on the wall
wondered why my aunt was weeping.

Blue Baby

They always tiptoed round the hole
until one day when I was twelve

they said I'd had a little sister.
Where is she now I asked.

In Heaven with the angels,
they replied. I was not convinced.

*She was a Blue Baby, bless her heart,
died when she was six days old.*

After that, trying to drift off to sleep
I'd see her floating in the air outside my window,
rippling arms the color of the sky, calling,
telling me I should've been the one to die.

You never told me, my dead sister
it's our family's grownups
who know how to splinter hearts with words
as blue and cold as ice.

The Alchemist

Uncle Gerald used to make wine
from mayhaw berries gathered
in Louisiana woods. He went among the trees
to escape Aunt Lola's nagging tones.

He would decant his brew,
range it in battalions of pop bottles
propped against the window.
It was bilious pink, the shade of Doris Day's lipstick.

He gave me a case. I stashed it in the cellar.
At night, the bottles would explode, one by one,
bayou fusillade. Finally I decided
things had gone far enough,

poured the last one down the drain.
The sink was stippled with rust-coloured stains
but when the mayhaw wine hit them,
they smoked, went fizzzzz, melted straight into air.

Poor Lola died quite suddenly
one evening after dinner.
Nobody was surprised.

Cottonmouth

Mama takes me fishing.
At dawn, we go out to the garden.
The earth is black,
writhing, full of purple worms.

We put them in a Mason jar,
set off in her two-tone Chevrolet.
On the radio, Hernando's Hideaway
sings tunes of dark secluded places.

We drive through haunted woods,
sun filtering down through
trees dripping Spanish moss,
ghostly beards of lost grandees.

Then we reach the river.
The Mermentau is thick and brown,
roiling currents whirl on the surface.
We take out cane poles, bait our hooks, wait.

When fish strike, the shock of impact
travels up my arm, electric current.
We haul them in, bream, perch,
the occasional tough old gar.

Mama holds the fish, threads a line through gills,
puts the stringer in the water at our feet. Suddenly
a thick coiled form rises up, primeval dragon
with a mouth of nightmare white.

The cottonmouth is biting at the fish.
I run into the forest shrieking.
My mother's made of sterner stuff.
With a stick, she beats the snake away, laughs, pulls out the fish.

That night, when we get home,
she cooks them for our dinner.
What about the poison, Mama? I ask.
Nothing can hurt us, honey, she replies.

Permanent Damage

My mother wanted a daughter with blonde ringlets.
My hair was wild and straight. She marched me off
to the beauty parlour. "Odile," she drawled in honeyed tones,
"can you give this child a permanent?"
Odile put in bristled rollers, stabbed me with bobby pins,
slapped acrid purple goop over my scalp,
the smell so strong it scorched my lids.
Like a doomed saint, I endured the fumes
for what seemed forever. Then Odile lathered,
rinsed, dried. In the mirror I saw a head,
twisting gorgon mane, cold burning eyes.

Closet

When I was a little girl
my mother's closet was
a cave of wonders.

In it dresses swirl,
smell of Chanel, caress my face.
One is white lace. Another, midnight satin shimmers,
pools smooth and slick.

On the floor, her shoes point out in spokes
of symmetry, go clock clock
when I stagger down the hall.

My favourite thing's a hat
made of brown loops with golden spangles
brittle vivacious crown.

Heaven

We thought those Grande Isle summers
would last forever. Louisiana corsair haven
full of golden treasure.

My cousin Martha and I go crabbing.
She holds the string, I dip the net.
We don't talk much. Two solemn pigtailed girls
intent upon our task. Heat beats down.

In the distance, Uncle John floats
out on the waves, spreads out X-shaped,
buoyed up by tractor tire. The waves go
hush hush hush against the shore.

The beach house is made of timber.
No running water. Aunt Mary boils and scrubs and cleans,
raises an eyebrow when my flighty mama
says to cousin Stevie let's go fish.

Mama's voice is low and sweet,
thick Mississippi honey. She and Stevie,
pirates both, conspirators.
They go out to the jetty, bait their hooks,

sit down to wait, legs dangling low.
Stevie, silent, straightens, motions to my mama,
points to his bending pole.
We strain to hear their voices

but the words are indistinct.
She puts her arm around his shoulders,
helps him reel in a silver squirming fish.
His grin could light the sky.

I don't know if I believe
in a Heaven full of wings and harps,
But if the Hereafter does exist,
I imagine it will be

Grand Isle with Uncle Johnny floating,
Aunt Mary bustling,
Martha and me crabbing,
Mama and Steve two pirates fishing.

All held, eternal in
warm golden Grand Isle light.

Trove

Clearing my mother's house,
I empty out her handbag, find

> a tasseled cigarette,
> a lipstick labeled Fire and Ice,
> a steno pad with cryptic scrawls
> a photograph of me aged five
>
> a tissue blotted with a kiss.

No Wonder I Hate Films.

I saw my first film with a lady
who took care of me,
Mrs. Pearson, English war bride.
She loved crochet and Hot Tea.

The film was called *The A-Bomb*.
I thought the theatre would blow up
that we'd flower out to doom
in radioactive sparks.

 I was five years old.
I pressed my fists against my eyes,
hid under the seat in the dark, shrieking.

Movies take me back
to looming death, dark floors, popcorn,
wads of gum and people's feet.

Rita the Walking Doll

When I was small I hated dolls.
My cousin Martha and I played with plastic horses.
They could run and kick and neigh,
escape prim Southern parlours,
never said Yes ma'am.

One Christmas morning, though, a doll was skulking there
beneath the tree when I went down the stairs.
Her dress was stiff red taffeta,
polka-dotted white. Her eyes stared into space.
Her legs moved back and forth, but never swayed.

I hated her on sight. Later, one December afternoon,
my cousins and I were cowboys and Indians.
I played, needless to say, Comanche,
declaring warpath just like on TV, blood-thirsting.

And smiling, I scalped Rita.

Petticoats

At square-dancing classes, under our skirts,
we wore petticoats
made of yards and yards of scratchy net.

We whirled and spun. *Allemand* left,
dos-si-dos swing your partner
fiddles dipped and wailed.

The boys tried their best to hold us tight,
foiled by acres of lethal ruffles.
We were prickly female hedgehogs,

encased in frothy chastity,
fending them off,
laughing.

Jesse Garon

The first time we went on stage,
I felt you there, dark shimmer
over my left shoulder.

I hold my guitar, feel your fingers on the strings
strumming hound dogs, rocking jails,
in now or never land.

In swirls of shrieking girls
your shadow stands, tall male mast
floating in white spotlight sails.

When the curtain falls, I go backstage,
see you lurking in my mirror,
try to blot you out

wonder if
you're lonesome tonight.

*Jesse Garon Presley was Elvis Aaron Presley's stillborn twin.

Ambrosia

Take two pounds of Florida oranges.
Peel, then segment carefully. Add a tale
from Aunt Cecile about her bastard husband Jack
who ran off with that floozy from the Coast.

Then take one coconut. Hurl its hairy head
against the floor. It will burst open, just like
the head of Janie's husband Number One
who put a pistol to his mouth.

Grate white snowflakes into a crystal bowl.
Presentation will be enhanced with a few drops
of knuckle gore. They will accent the flavor,
add a touch of pinkish elegance.

Shelling Peas

The afternoon is woven thick
with mauve wisteria scent,
the buzzing of cicadas. Across the street, hymns blare

from the Baptist church loudspeaker.
Rock of Ages, Blest for Me
Onward Christian Soldiers
On Grandmother's front porch,

we rock back and forth
shelling peas, sliding a thumbnail
down central seams of leathery green,
fanning out the skins.

Abide With Me
Although I Walk in Death's Dark Vale

Peas pop out, clatter in the bowl
like pirate coins as we continue rocking
back and forth, encased in sunlight,
death and war and crucifixions.

Err with Verve

I never could hold a note.
But that didn't stop me
from trying out for choir.

The Choirmistress,
starched Virginia matron
looks at me over gilded specs
as I caterwaul with gusto.

She smiles, says, "That's good, Susan:
Err with Verve."
Against all odds,
she lets me in.

Hurler

I went to college in some style
to the sort of place where young ladies
from good families could board their horse,
if they so wished.
In the second year, however,
Dad speculated on wheat futures
and circumstances changed.

I marked papers, babysat for profs,
waited tables in the dining hall, heard
lobotomized debutantes talk
of boys with bank accounts as future consorts
while looking straight through me.
This does encourage one
to develop a rather jaundiced view
of sisterhood.

On the last day of term I walked in
with a tray stacked 12-plate high
on my left shoulder.
Olympic discus thrower,
I demurely hurled the tray
in perfect arc, shattering titters, twitters.
Stunned silence followed.

Amid the fragments,
holding up both sides of skirts
I did a perfect three-point curtsey
as Southern ladies learn to do
from infancy, and topped it off with
patronizing windshield wiper wave,
queenly razor smile.

Bomb Threats

My very first job was teaching in an all-black school
in Avon, Mississippi (Home to the World's Meanest Rednecks)
in the year of desegregation.

1969. Separate but equal. What a laugh!
The white school had textbooks. We had none.
I taught them Spanish anyway.

With integration there were bomb threats.
The white kids had textbooks but no Spanish.
I told my students, *"No vamos a dejar*

que estos imbecilies nos asusten."
We won't let those morons scare us.
Not one single bit.

Flight Map

We judder westward through the night.
On screen a cartoon plane hops
over rivers, bays, Atlantic.

Squares mark shipwrecks:
    1864   Tecumseh
    1912   Titanic
    1915   Lusitania
    1941   Bismarck

Why the hell do airlines think
we'll find wrecks reassuring?

I think of you, my sister,
hope I'll arrive in time
before you reach that last horizon

wonder if you'll drop right off the edge,
spiral down the dark blue currents,
float among phosphorescent monsters
turn cartwheels in the deep

or sail off free and disappear
into the radiant night.

Etymology

Relating to or marking boundaries.
From *terminus*, end, boundary line.
Sense of *'situated at the extreme end"*
(of something), dates from 1805.
Meaning *fatal*, first recorded 1891.

By the time I get there, I hope you haven't
reached the terminal, my sister.
Hope your end is not extreme.
I remind myself that all our journeys
will arrive one day at that dark destination,

wonder what's on the other side,
if other side there is.

Taxi

The people from the hospice
give us a pamphlet. The dying,
it says, often speak of journeys,
cars, departures.

'Where's my taxi?' you ask,
your voice imperious.
'Why's it taking so long?'
I lie at your side, hold your hand.

'They're sending a special taxi,
just for you,' I say, voice brittle
but not breaking. 'Pink Cadillac,
Nat King Cole on the tape deck.'

Then I go to the screen porch
where friends have gathered.
Light flickers through the trees.
I smile, sip wine. You'd want

your friends and guests well tended,
Southern Lady to the end.
And when my back was turned
your taxi came.

Tightrope Walker

The little one was premature
and fragile. Tiny red starfish.
When she came home
from intensive care, her mother,
my daughter, got up
every two hours for months
to express breast milk,
walk the floor, sing lullabies,
change nappies, stroke her cheek,

walk the tightrope across the dark valley
bear her over into the light.

What Every Mother Knows

Most shadows are grape-coloured.
They have clear contours, pooling,
flowing violet in our wake,
made of just one piece.
Not mine. She's scythed in two.

Her left side holds the children close.
She tends the home fires, helps with homework,
bakes cakes, thinks of what she's missing:
bright lights, late nights, promotions,
sparkling conversations.

Her right half is strong, high-powerered.
She chairs meetings, sits on boards, conquers worlds,
thinks of her children's little triumphs,
their first words, steps taken
when she wasn't there.

Both frayed shadow halves have edges
sutured with a bloodstained needle,
limned with hues of dark grey longing
serrated by regret.

I Won't

I bring you red roses
sit on the wooden bench
look out over the valley.

You loved this view.
The wind ruffles my hair,
whispers in the grass.

I look down at my feet
see a sprinkle of forget-me-nots.
Rest assured, my love.

II.

Salem

Betty Parris

I don't want to play this game.
The room is dim. My father said
in the cemetery there are graves
for naughty children who forget
to say their prayers. In the moving shadows
Indians and witches lurk.

The big girls hold a glass up high,
egg yolk floating in the water, peer into its depths
to find out who they'll marry. Their voices flicker, dart.
In the candlelight, I peek around their elbows
see the spectre of a coffin, run shrieking from the room

try to flee the rising darkness.

George Parris

My greatest fear
was what parishioners would say,
when the girls choked and writhed,
shouted foul blasphemies.
When I came here, they did not want me.
They failed to see my eminence, their own luck.
When my Betty foamed and gibbered,
And niece Abigail screamed that
she was pricked by needles none of us could see,
I feared they'd blame it all on me.

Still: if the Devil targets me
makes these silly girls shudder, shriek,
grab burning brands straight from the hearth
and throw them in the air,
all this is evidence of my sanctity, my godliness.
I am their pastor, leader of God's Chosen People,
Satan's worthy foe, destined to build
the glowing City on a Hill,
here in this darkest wilderness.

Cotton Mather

When they tried the wizard Burroughs
and then sentenced him to hang,
they brought him in a cart to Gallows Hill.
He said a perfect Paternoster with the noose
around his neck. The crowd murmured,
shifted, said he could not be a wizard,
nearly set him free.

But I rode up on my pale horse,
said his ruin was for the greater good,
that he was chief of the dark forces
swarming in the air, sent to bring about our ruin.
So they muttered, slunk away.

I nodded to the hangman
to complete his task, smiled
as Burroughs danced his final jig,
prayed for his blackened soul.

Martha Carrier

They called me Queen of Hell.
What do they know,
these grim black scarecrows
gathered at my feet.

Why would I blight their crops,
send plagues to kill their cattle,
freeze the blood within their veins?
I laugh as they put the rope
around my neck, look down and say

if you want to behold evil
twisted bubbling black thing
spawned by Satan,
gaze into your own hearts,
look deep into each others' eyes.

Werewolf

We call him Peter Stumpp because he's lost a hand.
A farmer, a Respectable Man, a Pillar of the Village.
Or so we thought. But when the moon is full
he goes into the forest, puts on his magic belt. Black fur sprouts
down arms, legs, muzzle, belly. Fangs flash white.

Then he crouches outside in the shadows,
rips babies straight from wombs, savouring
these dainty morsels. He eats the brain of his own son.
But real proof comes when a wolf without a paw
is shot. Stubb denies all. Of course, we torture him,
force him to confess,

tear his flesh with pincers,
burn him at the stake. We can see
his heart is black, know he was a werewolf because
when we look at his remains through a dark glass,
we see our own face looking back.

Basilisk

It ripples toward us, head held high.
On its brow a bishop's mitre,
white deadly diadem. Its fiery breath
leaves ashes in its wake. Inexorable,

it undulates. Its stare splits stones.
It does not countenance dissent,
feels it contains the only Truth. Its gaze will petrify
all those who dare to disagree,

turn them to hard unfeeling bone
corseted tight in certainties.

Salamander

In the white heat
of the blaze the salamander writhes.
Flames lick around its scales,
embrace its glittering green eyes.

Its contortions lead us to believe
that it is dead, that its dance
in this infernal core has melted it
to glowing cinders, scrolls of ash.

But no. From molten heart
the salamander comes out strong and entire.
Popes give gold for capes of silver salamander skin
to ward off devils, shield them from the fire.

Lucy

In the painting, she's a young girl
with flowing chestnut hair. Her tunic
veils the swell of adolescent breasts.
Around her shoulders lies a russet velvet cloak.
In her hands she holds a plate
on which lie two eyes. Two fried eggs,
they gaze up at us mournfully.

When she said no to the suitor
chosen by her father, she was sentenced
to be ravished. Divine forces put a stop to that,
stopped ravening wolves straight in their tracks.
They tried to burn her then, gouged out her eyes.
The flames went out,leaving pale wisps of smoke.
Finallly, they pierced her heart,
killed her with a silver sword.

But she ended up with the last laugh.
This valiant girl, face pocked with empty sockets,
is known as Lucy, deliverer of maidens,
patron saint of light.

Jack Kipling's Medals Speak

We were meant to hang above his heart,
dazzle debutantes, daunt his peers,
prove his prowess and his strength

when he came marching home again
after taking part in this jolly lark,
this very Great Adventure.

Under glass, we glint. Three brothers.
Each of us thinks he's more distinguished,
more impressive, braver than the other two.

>On the left, I hang in tricolor,
>Napoleonic red, white, blue.
>Below me shine two stars, a sword.
>
>In the middle, I'm orange,
>flanked by blue and white.
>From me trails a gleaming manly profile.
>
>On the left, my rainbow colours stream.
>Dangling from me is a golden sun
>a young man trapped, immortal.

Now, while Batemans tourists gawk at us
safe in our glass case,
what's left of Jack lies shattered,
shredded, lost in Flemish soil.

They never knew just where,
because his face was blasted off.
Not much chest was left,
no uniform to hang us from.

Harriet Jacobs

My owner was obsessed with me.
He followed me, pawed me
in places where he shouldn't
when my mistress wasn't watching
and sometimes when she was.
To escape I loved another,
though he too was white.
My master would not let us marry,
would not free our children.

One day he pressed against me
panting like a dog, said he'd kill me
if I refused him. I shoved him off,
took refuge in an attic,
the space too small to stand.
I hid there in the dark for seven years.
Through slits between the floorboards
I could catch glimpses of my little ones
from time to time. Finally, I fled to the North.

I learn to read. I write the story of my life
for pink ladies in prim parlours,
show them I too am mother,
just like them, help them to see

the only one who owns my life,
is me.

Make America Great Again

We must come together now.
Grab 'em by the pussy.
Build that wall.
It can't happen here.

Grab 'em by the pussy.
Lock her up.
It can't happen here.
Swastikas painted on a wall.

Lock her up.
We won. Get over it.
Swastikas painted on a wall.
You'd be in jail.

We won. Get over it.
Nasty woman.
You'd be in jail.
If you're a star you can do anything.

Revenge

Back in the fifties, pet baby gators.
were in style. As time went by, they grew.
Cuteness faded as their teeth
grew longer, sharper.

A solution, though, was found:
      grab reptile by the tail
      suspend over toilet bowl
      flush out into the pipes.

Now, it's said, that gators thrive
in New York sewers. Albino predators,
they float in darkness, flourish, eating
our detritus. Their eyes glow yellow
in the murk of floating crap and condoms.

I love to think of their revenge:
      smug buttocks lower themselves, enthroned,
      when from the depths up swims
      this prehistoric monster, nightmare white.
      It surges forth, takes a quick bite.

III

Lines of Desire

We humans are anarchic creatures,
prone to hare off at wild tangents

> ignoring yellow lines
> crossing when the light is red
> walking over pristine grass
> taking shortcuts through dark alleys.

City planners factor this
into their blueprints, map the chaos,
predict unpredictability
while we mortal beings careen careless
on the green baize field of Fate,
shining snooker spheres colliding.

There's beauty in these desiring lines,
these wild asymmetries,
these awkward urgent angles.

Animal Magic

If I could be an animal, I'd be a lion.
Majestic, languid, letting out the occasional roar,
eating American dentists as an aperitif.

Or a panther, sleek and black.
Or a snowy owl, hovering over barns.
Or a lustruous, pampered widow's cat.

Or perhaps a racehorse running free,
or a seagull eating Big Macs, shitting on unwary tourists,
or a whale sounding to dark depths.

But on reflection,
there are no ifs, because
I am animal, and glad to be.

Even with all the lusts, and killings,
the being vulnerable to hunters
and to my own hungers.

A Bibliophile's Vision of Heaven

Room after room after room
of stories, lives bound in vellum
and gilded letters. The smell of dust

and leather. Slanting rays of sun
falling from high windows.
I lie back on a chaise longue

feet up, while a conga line of Clooneys
pours me goblets of fine champagne
and a legion of Clark Gables

fetches every book that takes my fancy.
My fingers caress their spines, savour their margins,
never stop at endings

Fundamental

I look over my shoulder
in the full-length mirror.
Coquettish catwalk pose.

Good child-bearing hips,
I've been told: Rubensian.
Dimpled, soft, rounded.

I'll never be Kate Moss
or Cara Delevigne.
No scrawny elegance for me, I fear.

I love the honesty of what is real,
of pink abundant flesh.
No photoshopping here.

Don'ts

Things not to say:

You're pretty well preserved for your age.
My wife doesn't understand me.
My ex/dead wife didn't understand me.
My ex/dead wife was the love of my life.
I have a few issues.
There's something I need to tell you.

But the killer line of all is this:
I love you for your mind.

Bordello

There's something risqué
about winter sunsets.
Black lace trees are filigree
on blue and pink sky satin,
lewd sexy colours.

Not an easy look to carry off with flair,
this joining up of lush and spare.

Kouros

There he lies, fallen god. Our Greek guide tells us
he was hewn there from the rock. When they went
to lift him up, they found a flaw and let him lie.
Children clamber on his face.
A fitting resting-place for sun-soaked god
of wine. He lies there smiling at the sky,
garlanded with lavender and thyme.

I touch his feet and find them warm,
earthed by his imperfections.

Greensleeves

The Tower has repelled invaders
for a thousand years. Now its gates
are breached by gawking hordes.
We queue up to buy tickets, trot
in docile rows behind Beefeater strides.
Our guide cracks jokes
tells tales of spilt entrails
laughs at squeamish shudders.

In the Chapel, he tells us
bones were found beneath the stone
and some belonged to Anne Boleyn.
When we ask could they be sure, he grins
oh yes she had six fingers
on one hand. When they said
she was a witch, she'd cover up
in flowing sleeves.

When we emerge the sun is cold and bright.
I hear faint echoes. Mocking laughter tickles
rippling daffodils. Among green leaves
the wind blows evanescent madrigals
upon a flute of bones bleached white.

The Peacock's Song

Juno stands on tiptoe, reaches to the sky
to touch my iridescent feathers
garlanded with starry eyes.
My jeweled plumage shimmers, floats
down to the forest floor.

She tells me not to envy nightingales,
even though they fill the night
with shimmering clouds of notes
and I am left alone with my harsh cry.

Heart: An Assay

A radio station that plays cheesy pop songs
        You've lost that lovin' feeling
        Anyone who had a heart

A organ that pumps blood.
        Four dark red Blubebeard chambers
        Hollow contracting caves.

The centre of emotion
        My head says no but my heart says yes
        In major decisions, follow your heart

The essence
        The heart of the matter
        At heart, he's really kind

Without screens or masks or subterfuge
        which is what we all strive for: to speak
        to our beloved, heart to heart.

Under the Volcano

In the distance, Mt. Etna rises,
summit veiled in smoke
and clouds. Below, fields ripple out,
fold into deep blue valley.

I sit at a café on the square.
Passegiata crowds surge and swirl.
Two men strum plaintive mandolins.
At a nearby table, a tourist reads his news.

Bold headlines blare and blast,
boast of regained sovereignty.
It all seems so remote here
on this island in the sun.

I look to the horizon,
feel beneath my feet
the trembling ground,
the coming rain of liquid fire.

Palimpsest

The old Greek gods are written
in our sinews, sing in our blood.
Our lips draw tight in Cupid bows.
Our eyes hold rainbow Irises.

Atop our spine, the Atlas vertebra
holds up our weighty skull, globe balanced
on a butterfly of bone. Below, the mount of Venus
rises resplendent, conceals Hymen's shielded door.

Achilles heeled, we think we're armed against it all,
fire our arrows, garland ourselves in light,
climb peaks, think that the gods
will never let us fall.

Regrets

It's not the living
that gets you in the end.
It's the holding back,

the dares not taken,
the men I could have loved,
the races that I didn't run.

Among my very few regrets
are not the many things I did
but those I left undone.

Mixed Border

People speak of English country gardens
as idyllic spaces where we go
to escape from news
of crashing currencies,
armed strife, oil spills.
What do they know.

Mixed borders are war zones,
where peonies slug Sweet Williams.
Loutish lupins elbow tulips, bash buddleias.
Geraniums gouge sweet peas,
trip up alliums. Daffodils duke it out
with delphiniums and daisies.

Darwinian dystopias,
botanical Jerry Springers,
reality where only the strongest
and most ruthless will prevail.

Knowing

Learned scientists have shown
children play for reassurance
so we can learn to deal
with all those things we can't control.

Not an easy lesson. Still, in blindman's buff,
we hold hands out and stagger toward the void.
In hide and seek we crouch there

in the dark, waiting to be found
or not. We don't know when a ball
will curve and hit us in the face.

There's a strange elation in not knowing
whether we'll come back to the light
or fall cartwheeling into space.

Way Out

At a certain age, one starts to think
about the way we'd like
to leave this Vale of Tears.

No slow drip of poison to our veins.
No exploding planes.
It would be far more fun

to go in burst of glory,
frolicking with a lover
heart to heart, skin to skin,

or topple over dancing
under the glitterball, lights flashing,
drums pounding in our ears.

or fade to gentle night when sitting on a beach
smiling, waves
flowing in out, in out,

out.

Churchgoer

My pew's a blue bench looking out
on ancient woodland. The arched ceiling
glows, spinning with the seasons:

> in summer, green mosaic, sunlight-spangled
> in autumn, fiery vaults, hornbeam-ribbed,
> in winter, bright spare bones, gray-ceilinged.

In spring, bluebell clouds bring hope
of growth and resurrection.

About the Author

Susan Castillo Street is Harriet Beecher Stowe Professor Emerita, King's College London. She has published two collections of poems, *The Candlewoman's Trade* (Diehard Press, 2003), *Abiding Chemistry*, (Aldrich Press, 2015), and a pamphlet, *Constellations* (Three Drops Press, 2016). Her poetry has appeared in *Southern Quarterly*, *Prole*, *The High Window*, *Ink Sweat & Tears*, *Messages in a Bottle*, *The Missing Slate*, *Clear Poetry*, *Three Drops from a Cauldron*, *Foliate Oak*, *The Yellow Chair Review*, *Poetry Shed*, *The Lake*, *Picaroon*, *Atrium*, *The Fat Damsel*, *The Writers' Cafe* and other journals and anthologies.

Thanks to the Sticks Poets (Louisa Campbell, Sarah Miles, Lawrence Wilson, Sian Thomas, Jessica Mookherjee, and Jill Munro) and to the pirates of the Coast of Bohemia, for their excellent critical feedback and for their friendship.

#0239 - 280218 - C0 - 229/152/5 - PB - DID2135080